AF350998

She-Wolf Sonnet

Books by Cheryl Cantafio

MY STAY WITH THE SISTERS: POEMS

A PLACE NO FLOWERS GROW

BARRY AND THE BIG JUMP

(*November 2024*)

For those who love old-fashioned monster stories.

Copyright © 2024 by Cheryl Cantafio

All rights reserved. No part of this book may be used or reproduced in any manner whatsoever without written permission from the author except in the case of brief quotations embodied in critical articles and reviews.

This is a work of fiction. Names, characters, businesses, places, events, locales, and incidents are either the products of the author's imagination or used in a fictitious manner. Any resemblance to actual persons, living or dead, or actual events is purely coincidental.

Cover Design: Doni Waikel

ISBN: 979-8-9880452-5-0

First print edition 2024
Printed in the United States

She-Wolf Sonnet

by

Cheryl Cantafio

One: Him

Did you hear that beautiful song? That howl?

My body ached and quaked with every note.

That alluring call to fate run afoul.

I felt her warm breath dance across my throat.

That music belonged to a wild woman.

I loved the ferocity in her eyes.

That mischievous glint is where I began

To feel my stomach fill with butterflies.

Electric, magnetic, love at first sight.

That is not quite how it happened for us.

She stalked me in the dark by a street light.

Her feigned innocent approach treacherous.

I whistled along to the she-wolf's song.

Its rapacious chorus so right, so wrong.

Two: Her

He walked to his brownstone without a care.

He was a tower I wanted to scale.

I quickened my pace, exhaled a prayer.

And transformed into a human female.

We locked eyes and he never stood a chance.

I read every salacious thought he had.

I seduced him, enslaved him with my trance.

I smiled, bit my lip, and it drove him mad.

My pace slowed as his heavy steps quickened.

I could smell the lust leaking from his pores.

He was hungry instead of fear-stricken.

For curvy bodies he'd get on all fours.

I delighted in his throbbing heartbeat.

His pursuit of me a damned bloody treat.

Three: Him

She was like no other woman I knew.

Eyes amber, hair tousled, and arms limber.

Sinewy, adorned in a sapphire blue.

She said hello with a lupine timber.

An unnatural courage stirred in me.

I wanted to know every inch of her.

Fierce specimen, self-possessed and carefree.

My words poured freely and I felt hope stir.

She agreed to dine with me the next day.

Her smile faltered when she saw the full moon.

Its silvery cold light tore her away.

My only solace was I'd see her soon.

The adrenaline left my body tired.

Sleep was the sole lover I desired.

Four: Her

I made it to the woods, seconds to spare.

My skin tore from my elongated bones.

My tailored dress now ratty and threadbare.

I bayed and vibrated with all its tones.

I am the one who caused night terrors.

My appetite did not discriminate.

I feasted on saints and philanderers.

Lycanthropy ruptured my moral gate.

The loneliness of this life weighed on me.

Its curse a heavy weather-worn fur coat.

I longed for a lover to stay not flee.

I feared being a flitting anecdote.

The curse denied what my human heart craved.

My calamity kept me ill-behaved.

Five: Him

I awoke to shrieks that traveled my spine.

A discovery of bodies mangled.

I needed to know she was safe, a sign.

I prayed she wasn't dead or entangled.

It's as though the universe read my heart.

Her sad amber eyes found mine at the scene.

A silent vow to never be apart.

She was a vision in emerald green.

All shrank from the girl who found the two dead.

Horror, madness, fear etched on her face.

Warbling *Am I next* with each tear she shed.

Danger left the scene sparse of clue or trace.

Something scratched at the corners of my mind.

I watched my love's bewildered face unwind.

Six: Them

I knew my signature strike, my kill tells.

I prided myself on a clean demise.

While these murders held certain parallels,

There were two of us, one wolf in disguise.

I derailed from my train of deep thought.

And nuzzled into his open embrace.

He produced two garden tickets he bought,

My stomach hoped for a good dinner place.

I grappled with the full moon's chokehold.

He too appeared spellbound by her beauty.

We walked through a maze of marigold.

Antagonized by her call to duty.

The night called to us and we answered it.

It punctured our souls as our bodies split.

Seven: We/Werewolves

Long-buried instincts placed into motion.

Pulled us, catapulted us, to the brink.

Our musky scents were a magic potion.

We unsheathed our fangs, but they didn't sink.

Dumbstruck why neither of us suspected,

Disparate pack members in one place rare.

Souls psychically interconnected.

Lonely and shared a similar prayer.

We were feral creatures of the full moon.

We rejoiced in creating our own pack.

We slept in flower beds and woke at noon.

Unsuspected lovers on the attack.

Mistress Moon's cycle ceased without fanfare.

We continued our human love affair.

Eight: Epilogue

We became the town's dark folklore for years.

They made an informal accord with us:

Their criminal contingent disappears,

We the night creatures could live without fuss.

Humans aren't known to keep promises though.

Word spread quickly of the town's protectors.

Fear consumed the young girl from long ago.

Some were hunters and some were collectors.

We had a lovely long lunar-filled life.

We assumed our much older, grayer forms.

When a man's silver bullet killed my wife,

I made songs with his death screams during

storms.

If you hear a mournful howl, it's for her.

Each note is for my beautiful monster.

Acknowledgments

Thank you to Doni Waikel for adding to the atmosphere of the book with her book cover design.

Thank you to R. B. Wood and *Sudden Fictions Podcast*. The *howl* prompt was irresistible.

I am forever grateful to friends Julie Shaw and Tami Osborne for reading anything I throw their way. Thanks for cheering me on to keep writing.

And thank you, dear readers, for taking a chance on a werewolf-themed sonnet. (Shakespeare and Marlowe are somewhere shaking their heads.)

What is a sonnet?

The sonnet is a popular classical form that has compelled poets for centuries. Traditionally, the sonnet is a fourteen-line poem written in iambic pentameter, employing one of several rhyme schemes, and adhering to a tightly structured thematic organization. The name is taken from the Italian *sonetto*, which means "a little sound or song." (Information source: https://poets.org/glossary/sonnet)

I followed the Shakespearean sonnet format: three quatrains and a couplet follow this rhyme scheme: *abab, cdcd, efef, gg*. (Information source: https://poets.org/glossary/sonnet)

About the Author

Cheryl Cantafio is a poetry and children's book writer from Norristown, Pennsylvania. When she's not writing, she works in information technology, co-hosts a podcast (*You Only Go Once*), reads gothic horror or thriller novels, or binge-watches movies and television series. Her book *My Stay with the Sisters: Poems* was her debut as an author and poet in May 2023. Her gothic poetic tale, *A Place No Flowers Grow*, released in September 2024. *Barry and the Big Jump* will be her debut children's book, set to release in November 2024.

Connect with Cheryl on:

- Instagram: @cherylc.writer

- Website: https://www.cherylcantafio.com

www.ingramcontent.com/pod-product-compliance
Lightning Source LLC
Chambersburg PA
CBHW071255140726
47996CB00007B/2851